THE FUN BOOK OF CARTOON FACES · 

Blitz®

9   8   7   6   5   4   3   2   1

Digit on the right indicates the number of this printing

Library of Congress Cataloging-in-Publication Number 98-66889

ISBN 0-7624-0452-3

This book may be ordered by mail from the publisher.
Please include $2.50 for postage and handling.
**But try your bookstore first!**

Running Press Book Publishers
125 South Twenty-second Street
Philadelphia, Pennsylvania 19103-4399

**Visit us on the web!**
**www.runningpress.com**

If you are interested in ordering Bruce Blitz Video Kits, please visit your local
arts and crafts store, or send for a video kit catalog:
Blitz Art Products
P.O. Box 8022
Cherry Hill, NJ 08002
USA

THE

# FUN BOOK

## OF CARTOON

# FACES

By
BRUCE BLITZ

RUNNING PRESS
PHILADELPHIA · LONDON

# CONTENTS

## PART I
## INSTRUCTION

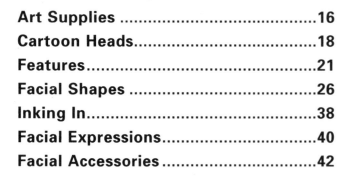

## PART 2
## ACTIVITIES

## ABOUT THE AUTHOR

Bruce Blitz started out as the boy who drew funny pictures of the principal at school. Now he appears at numerous school assembly programs and demonstrates his cartooning skills to rave reviews from everyone (including the principal!). He has been drawing professionally for more than twenty years.

Blitz is the creator and host of the internationally aired television series *Blitz on Cartooning*, which has earned four Emmy award nominations. He has authored several instructional books on drawing, produced a series of instructional drawing videos, and has appeared on a bunch of television programs, including *The Joan Rivers Show*, Discovery Channel's *Start to Finish*, and the QVC Shopping Network. Blitz is mostly self-taught, thanks to his experience in a wide variety of artistic fields. He has operated his own animation company in Philadelphia and Las Vegas, where he produced cartoon television commercials and animated sequences.

An accomplished, professional musician performing on both piano and organ, Blitz wrote the music for his television show and all of his instructional videos. The music from *Blitz on Cartooning* was even nominated for an Emmy! He is also noted for his caricature work, having appeared nationwide at trade shows, conventions, vacation resorts, and the 1982 World's Fair in Knoxville, Tennessee. He was born in Philadelphia, Pennsylvania, and now resides in Cherry Hill, New Jersey, with his wife and two children.

# HOW TO USE THE COVER OF THIS BOOK

Lay a piece of tracing paper over a wacky face
you created on the cover, and trace away!

8

**You can have a *wheel* good time with the cover while traveling in a car . . .**

. . . or on a plane.

**A cartoonist talks about the latest
and greatest art supplies,**

**and swaps gags and stories
with other cartoonist friends . . .**

## . . . and draws a lot!

Most importantly,
a cartoonist tries
to see humor in
everyday situations.

**A cartoonist can help deliver a message . . .**

**. . . and deliver a joke.**

**After lots of practice, a cartoonist can even begin to draw things for money!**

I guess you could say being a cartoonist makes you feel special.

## PART I

# ·INSTRUCTION·

NOW IT'S TIME TO LEARN WHAT IT TAKES
TO DRAW GREAT CARTOON FACES!

## ART SUPPLIES

You will need a pad of drawing paper or an inexpensive pad of newsprint. Plain old copy machine paper also works well. You will find that a pad of tracing paper comes in handy, too.

An eraser is necessary to make changes and to clean up your final sketch.

ERASER

You can use a black marker with a medium point to complete your drawing.

# CARTOON HEADS

Let's get started by drawing some cartoon heads. It all begins with shapes. When you draw shapes for your comic heads, be loose!

## IMPORTANT TIP:
DON'T TRY TO DRAW YOUR SHAPE WITH ONE FIRM, SINGLE PENCIL LINE. INSTEAD, AFTER THE PENCIL SKETCH IS COMPLETED, FINISH IT OFF WITH MARKER AND THEN ERASE THE PENCIL LINES!

## STEP 1

Make a swirly oval shape with your pencil in hand, but don't actually touch the pencil point to the paper . . . just get the loose flowing motion going round and round.

## STEP 2

When you are satisfied with the direction which your hand is going, simply lower the pencil point lightly to the paper while keeping the pencil circling. And there it is . . . a loosely drawn shape!

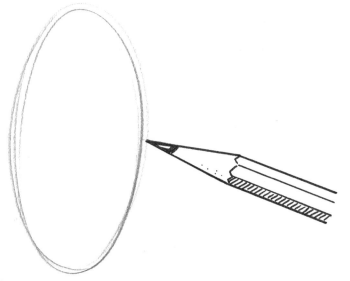

**Here's an example of an oval that was drawn by holding the pencil too tightly and bearing down on the point too hard.**

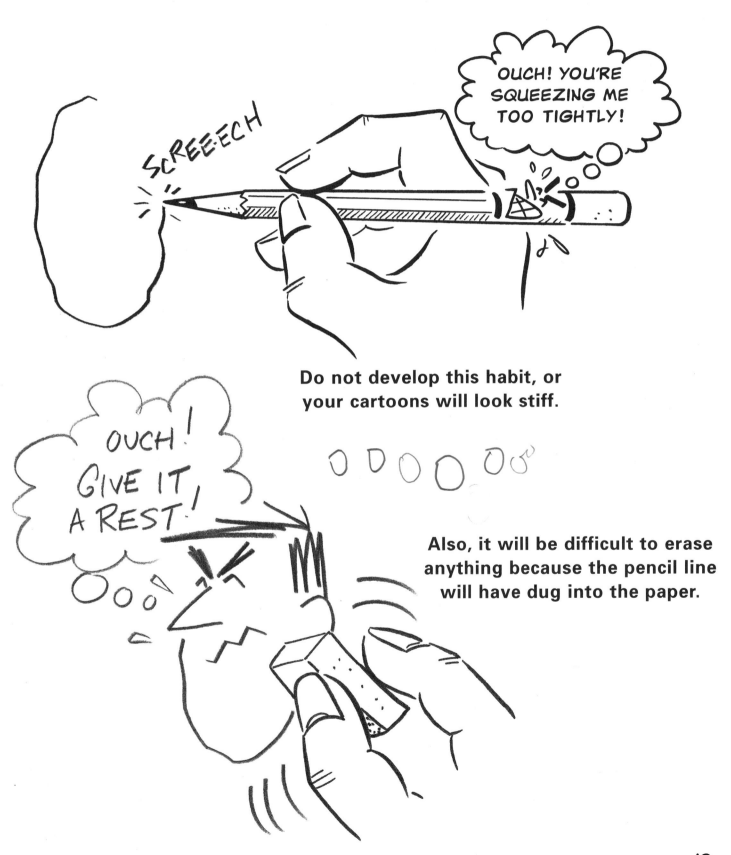

**Do not develop this habit, or your cartoons will look stiff.**

**Also, it will be difficult to erase anything because the pencil line will have dug into the paper.**

# LET'S SEE WHAT IT TAKES TO DRAW A CARTOON HEAD.

Now that you have your loosely drawn shape, let's draw two guidelines—one across and one down—that will help you place the features on the face.

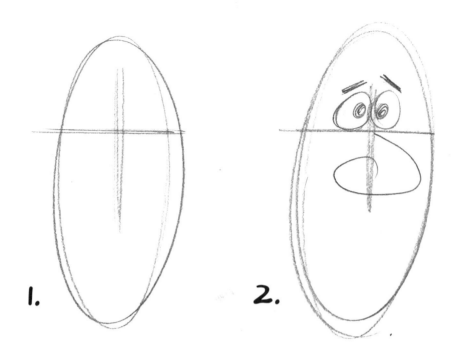

Next, add eyes, nose, mouth, ears, and hair.

And that's all there is to it!

# FEATURES

Before we move on to all of the shapes that you can use to create cartoon heads, let's explore cartoon features. You can practice these on a separate sheet of paper.

## EYES

# NOSES

**Side view**

**Front view**

# MOUTHS

**Front view**

**Side view**

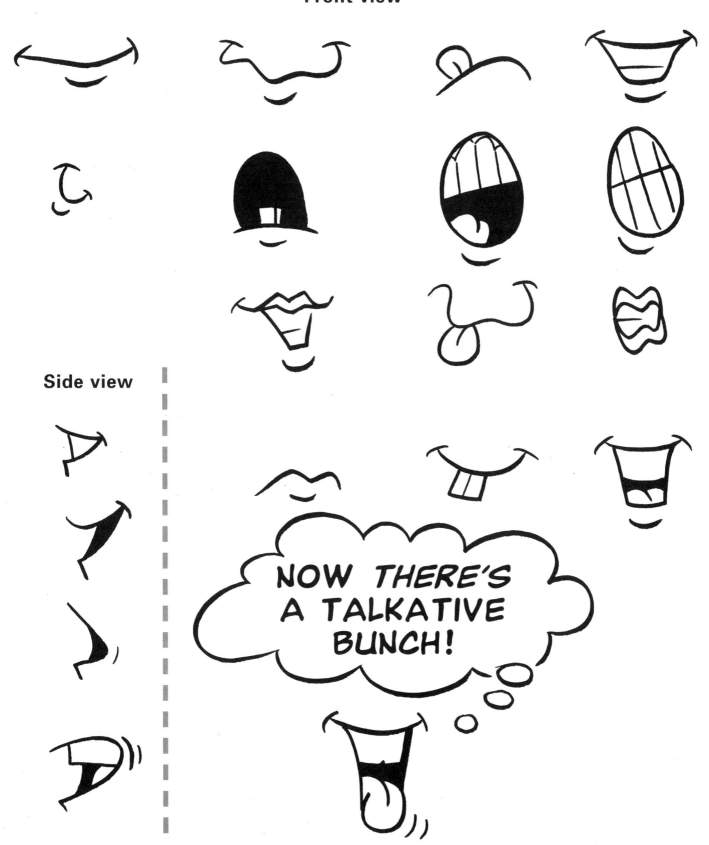

NOW *THERE'S* A TALKATIVE BUNCH!

# FACIAL OUTLINES, HAIR, AND EARS

As you can see on the cover of this book, different faces begin with different outlines.

# FACIAL SHAPES

By using basic shapes, we can create a variety of cartoon characters.

 **CIRCLE** Always start by very lightly drawing in your guidelines—across and down.

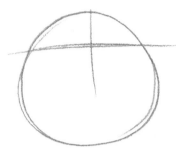 

**LONG RECTANGLE** Make sure you erase the guidelines when you're done!

. . . Now turn it upside down!

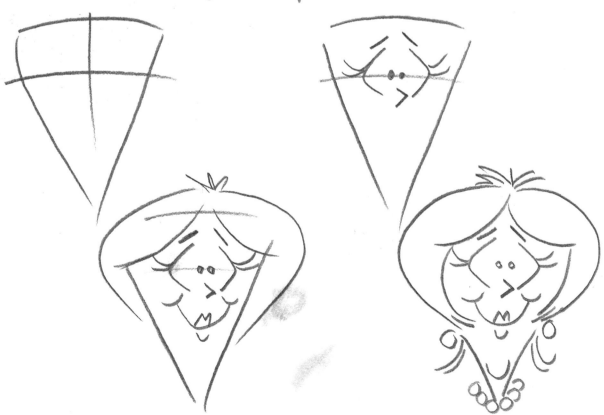

27

# SPHERE

Think of the oval shape you begin with as a three-dimensional object . . . like a balloon . . . and then wrap the guidelines around it to create a sphere.

**LEFT**　　　**RIGHT**　　　**UP**　　　**DOWN**

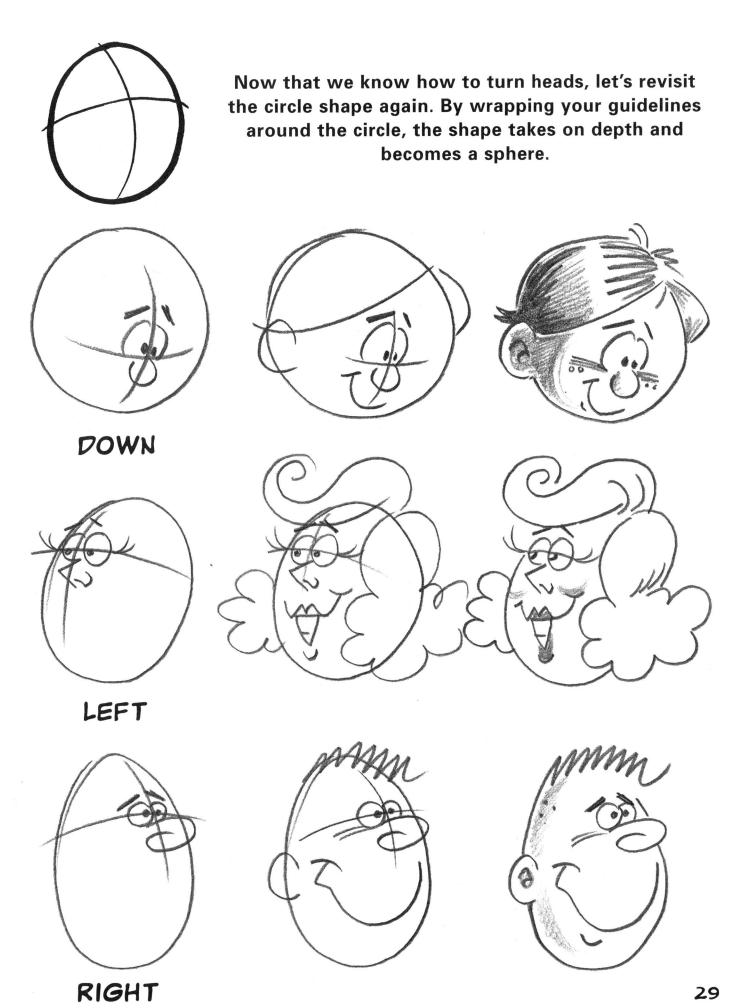

Now that we know how to turn heads, let's revisit the circle shape again. By wrapping your guidelines around the circle, the shape takes on depth and becomes a sphere.

DOWN

LEFT

RIGHT

# OVAL

This is a sphere that is elongated. It creates additional possibilities for cartoon faces.

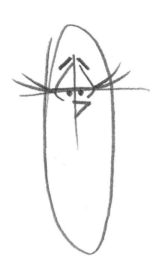

## TEARDROP

This shape is also a sphere, but with the top "pinched" to form a teardrop.

**Do you see how different shapes help you create different characters?**

WAH

**From a teardrop . . . to something that produces teardrops!**

**Why not reverse the last shape to create more variety?**

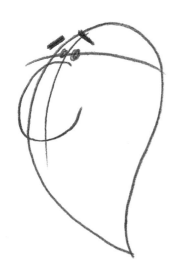

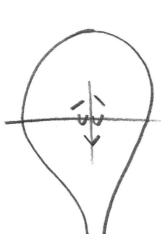

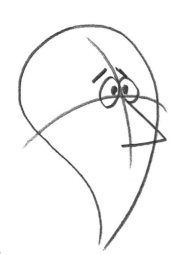

# TRIANGLE

Notice that once the face is established from this triangle, the points at the top and bottom are rounded to create a more pleasing comic face. This is where your eraser and marker come in handy.

# OVERSTUFFED BOOMERANG

Let's use this shape to draw a few side-view characters.

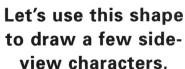

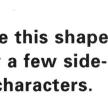

You can draw your cartoon face on either side of the shape for more variety, as in these two examples.

## CYLINDER

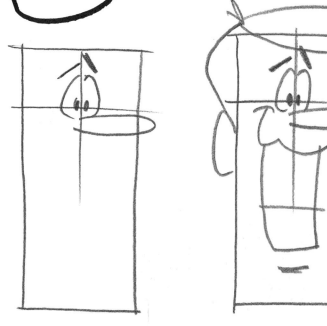

This is a square shape when seen straight on.

A COFFEE CUP IS A CYLINDER SHAPE . . . JUST LIKE ME.

But when it's tilted, a cylinder can have an oval on the bottom!

34

# DIAMOND

A diamond is really just two triangles joined together to form this great shape for cartooning.

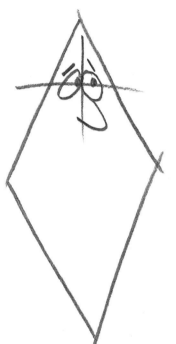

Comic heads that are built on a diamond usually have "pinchable" cheeks.

# PEANUT

This could also be called a "guitar" shape. It's as if you took a balloon and squeezed it around the middle.

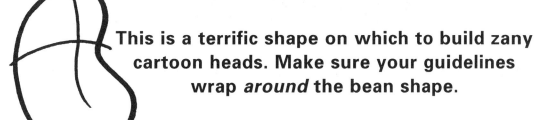

# BEAN

This is a terrific shape on which to build zany cartoon heads. Make sure your guidelines wrap *around* the bean shape.

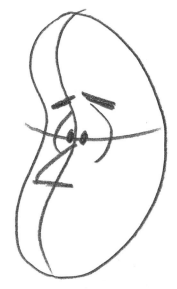

**ELONGATED**

**ROUNDED**

HEAR THAT FELLAS? WE'RE TERRIFIC SHAPES FOR CARTOONING!

# INKING IN

It's about time to learn the basic steps of inking-in your cartoons.

l. Draw your cartoon in pencil—very lightly— and use your eraser to make changes.

2. When you are satisfied, go over your pencil line with your marker, making one clean, definite line.

3. When the marker has dried, erase the entire drawing. The pencil line will be gone and the ink line will stay!

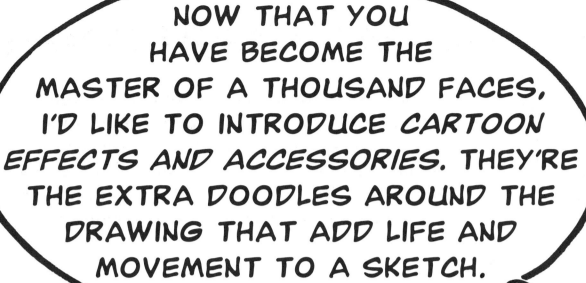

# FACIAL EXPRESSIONS

The next thing to learn is that all cartoon characters aren't always happy and smiling (as on the previous pages). They, too, have feelings! You as the cartoonist have to draw the appropriate expression to fit the situation your character is in. Here are some examples:

**WORRIED**          **WONDERING**          **HUNGRY**

**DAZED**          **CRYING**          **BAD TASTE**

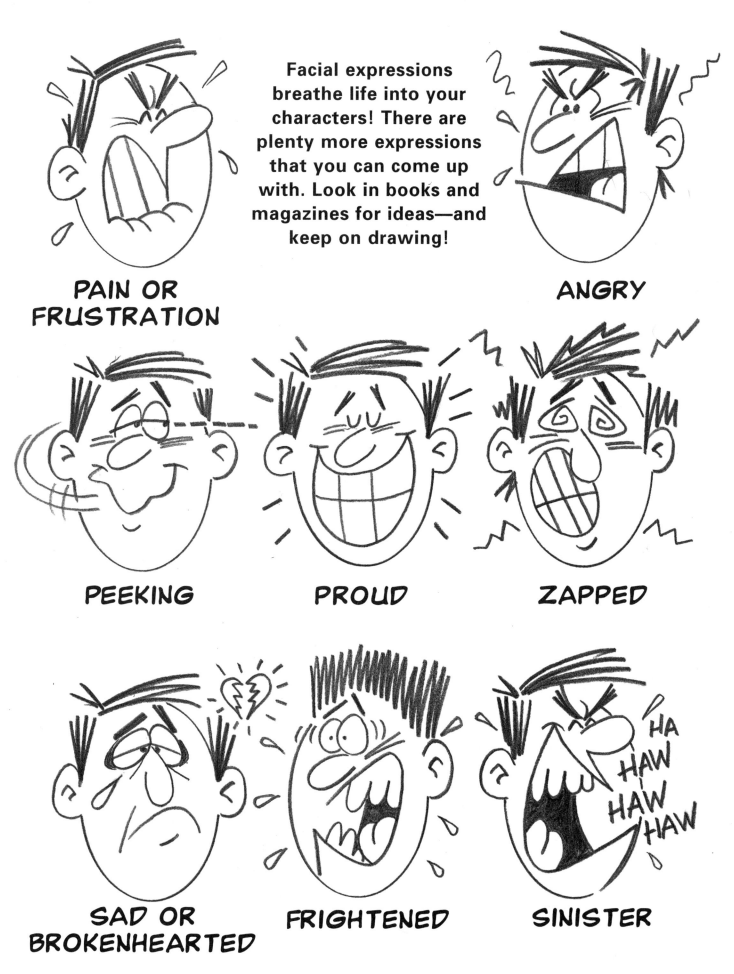

Facial expressions breathe life into your characters! There are plenty more expressions that you can come up with. Look in books and magazines for ideas—and keep on drawing!

**PAIN OR FRUSTRATION**

**ANGRY**

**PEEKING**

**PROUD**

**ZAPPED**

**SAD OR BROKENHEARTED**

**FRIGHTENED**

**SINISTER**

HA HAW HAW HAW

Turn to page 90 to find a fun activity using these expressions.

# FACIAL ACCESSORIES

Here are even more ways to add variety. Just look how much people differ from one another when you add little extra bits of personal expression.

# BEARDS AND MUSTACHES

CIRCUS
STRONGMAN

MAN FROM THE
EARLY 1900s

PROFESSOR
OR SCIENTIST

**Facial hair helps the reader see who the character is.**

THIS GUY
LOOKS A BIT
SUSPICIOUS.

A GOATEE
AND MUSTACHE
(WITH A BERET)
ESTABLISH THIS
FELLA AS
AN ARTIST.

RECOGNIZE
THIS MAN?

HEY, IT'S
ONLY ME
WITH MY NEW
MUSTACHE.

A FLUFFY WHITE
BEARD AND MUSTACHE
MAKES SANTA!

For this character, you can leave out the mouth because it's hidden under his mustache!

5 O'CLOCK SHADOW

STUBBLE

Two Different Ways to Draw a Man Who Needs a Shave

A "straggly" beard and mustache. This character looks like he has been shipwrecked on a deserted island for years!

A well-tailored, long, drooping mustache makes this guy look like an officer from the Civil War or a rich Southern gentleman.

# HATS

**It's important to draw hats that appear to fit *around* the head. That is, the head should look like it fits *inside* the hat.**

## LET'S DRAW A COWBOY HAT.

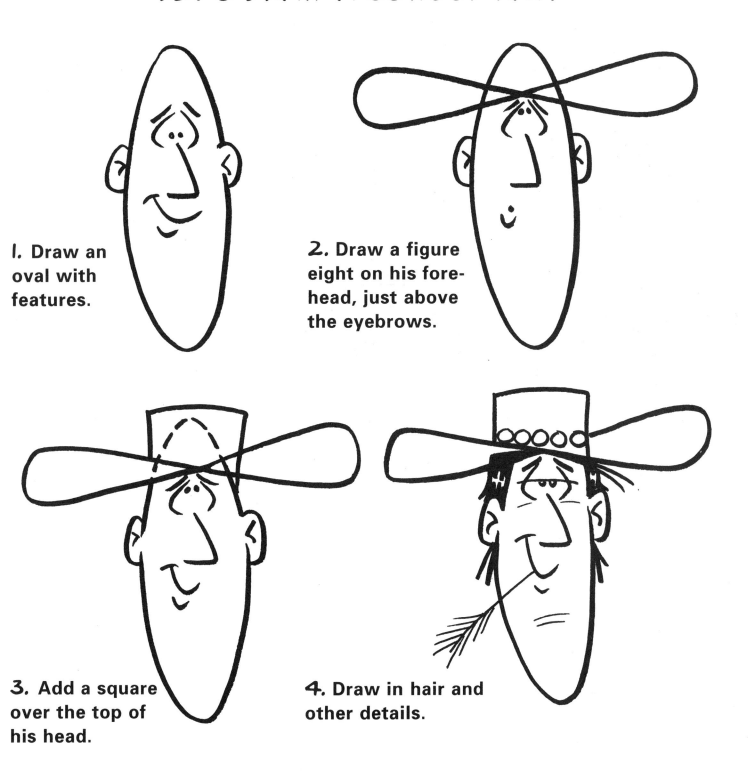

**I.** Draw an oval with features.

**2.** Draw a figure eight on his forehead, just above the eyebrows.

**3.** Add a square over the top of his head.

**4.** Draw in hair and other details.

DRAW A TOP HAT THE SAME WAY YOU DREW A COWBOY HAT. (PRETTY SPIFFY, HUH?)

A cone shape is all you need to draw a clown's hat.

BASEBALL HAT

A pith helmet for a safari . . . (coconut is optional)

ARMY HELMET

SKIER'S HAT

## FLOWER HAT
Overdone to emphasize a specific cartoon type. (Notice the bee?)

## HIGH-FASHION HAT WITH A VEIL

## STRAW HAT
It's not necessary to draw each weave of the straw . . . just indicate the texture here and there.

## FEATHER HAT
The guy sneezing is only there to squeeze out a little extra humor. (Not for him, though!)

AH-CHOO

# GLASSES

## Three Different Ways to Utilize Comic Glasses

EYES
SHOWING

EYES NOT
SHOWING

SUNGLASSES

DRAW LITTLE *WINDOWS*
TO INDICATE SHINE.

SOME MORE EXAMPLES.

RIDDLE:
WHAT'S THIS?

NO, IT'S NOT THE LETTER "J"
THAT HAS FALLEN DOWN . . .

ANSWER:
IT'S A SIDE
VIEW OF A PAIR
OF GLASSES.

# MISCELLANEOUS ACCESSORIES

FRECKLES

SWEATBAND

BONNET

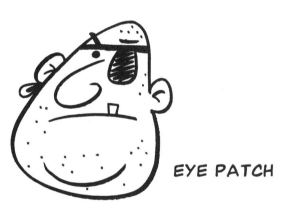

EYE PATCH

If you're "married to" the idea of drawing a scarf, make
sure you "tie the knot" in the back!

SCARF ON THE HEAD
(WITH EARRINGS)

SCARF OVER
THE MOUTH

**Practice using these accessories on Ed's Head, page 94**

# CARTOON TYPES

As the cartoonist, you are responsible for casting the right characters for your cartoon scene, just like casting actors for a movie or a play. In order to look the part, your characters must have the appropriate props, tools of the trade, and clothing.

## SCHOOL TEACHER

**STRICT-TYPE SCHOOL TEACHER**

**KINDLY TEACHER**

**TEACHERS HAVE:**

- RULERS
- BLACKBOARDS
- DESKS
- CHALK
- GLASSES
- APPLES

# DOCTORS

By varying the props and setting for this character, he or she can easily become a pharmacist or a laboratory worker.

## DOCTORS HAVE:

- DIPLOMAS
- STETHOSCOPES
- REFLEX HAMMERS
- TONGUE DEPRESSORS
- WHITE COATS
- PATIENTS
- WAITING ROOMS

TAP

SPROING

# OPERA SINGERS

**The robust form of this character provides much humor.**

**OPERA SINGERS HAVE:**

- LARGE OPEN MOUTHS
- FLOWERS
- MUSICAL NOTES
- AUDIENCES
- STAGE AND CURTAINS
- GOWNS AND TUXEDOS
- HAND MOVEMENTS

DO RE MI

LA LA LA LA LA LA LA

# SCIENTISTS

**As you can see below, scientists can be the brainy, quiet kind, or the sinister, wild, villainous type.**

### SCIENTISTS HAVE:

- BLACKBOARDS WITH MATHEMATICAL EQUATIONS
- TEST TUBES AND BEAKERS
- PUFFS OF SMOKE
- WILD HAIR
- LAB COATS
- WILD-EYED EXPRESSIONS WITH SINISTER LAUGHTER (MAD TYPE ONLY, PLEASE)
- BUSHY EYEBROWS

## TIMID AND STUDIOUS

## MAD SCIENTIST

# CHEFS

When you put the chef hat on a character, the reader knows instantly that he is a chef.

Try this . . .
Turn the number
"5" into a chef!

**CHEFS HAVE:**

- POTS AND PANS
- WHITE UNIFORM
- SPOONS AND LADLES
- NECK SCARF
- CHEF HAT
- STOVES
- MUSTACHE
- STEAM AND BUBBLES
- FOOD

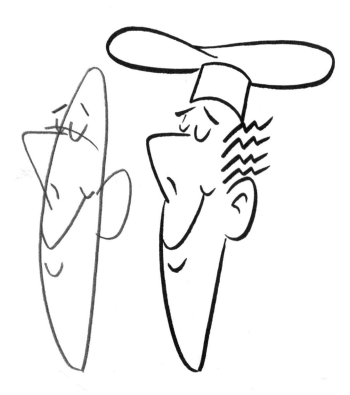

# GLAMOROUS WOMEN

**Learn to draw this type and you can cast her as a movie actress or a model.**

**GLAMOROUS WOMEN HAVE:**

- •EXPRESSIVE EYES
- •FANCY HAIR STYLES
- •FANS AND PHOTOGRAPHERS
- •BIG SMILES
- •EARRINGS
- •SPOTLIGHTS

**When drawing dark hair, leave some white gaps to indicate highlights.**

# TELEVISION PERSONALITIES

These characters could be cast as news reporters,
game show hosts, or talk show hosts.

## TELEVISION PERSONALITIES HAVE:

- BIG, WHITE TEETH
- CAMERAS
- MICROPHONE
- FLUFFY HAIR
- STRONG CHINS
- BIG SMILES
- BRIGHT SUITS
- SCRIPT OR NOTES

KINDLY OLD KING

SNOBBISH QUEEN

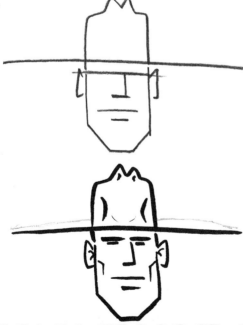

STATE TROOPER OR
FOREST RANGER

KARATE EXPERT

# ZANIES

**The sky is the limit when creating zany characters, because there are no rules. The sillier the better!**

IS THIS GUY HAVING A BAD HAIR DAY, OR WHAT?

## ONION-HEAD GUY

**Vary the size of each eyeball, and have the pupils look in different directions for that "wild-eyed" appearance.**

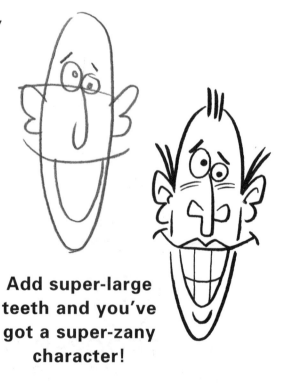

**Add super-large teeth and you've got a super-zany character!**

## CHARACTERS WITH CHARACTER

The following are examples of older and more "stylized" types.

This bearded and toothless fella looks like he could be a nutty old gold prospector with a hearty laugh.

This grim-looking guy could be a crotchety old hermit, a mean old landlord, or a cheap old miser.

**Drawing an exaggerated chin and straggly hair makes a great "old woman" cartoon character.**

**Here we have a sweet "grandmotherly" type . . . the kind that bakes cookies.**

# BABIES

**For babies, all the facial features are positioned low on the head.**

**FRONT**          **SIDE**

**The best way to make a character appear young is to draw the chin small and close to the mouthline.**

**3/4 VIEW**

**BABIES HAVE:**

•STUBBY FINGERS
•LITTLE OR NO NECK
•SHORT ARMS IN
RELATION TO THE REST
OF THE BODY

# LET'S SHOW HOW THEY GROW!

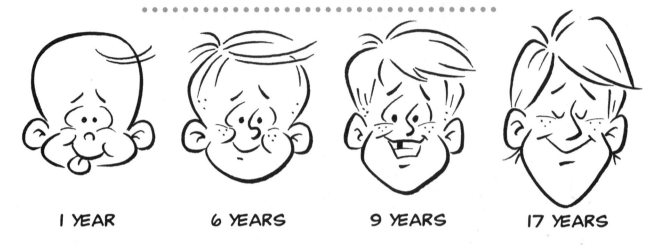

| 1 YEAR | 6 YEARS | 9 YEARS | 17 YEARS |

**The longer the chin is drawn, the older your character becomes!**

| 30 YEARS | 45 YEARS | 60 YEARS | 75 YEARS |

## HEY, LOOK AT THIS! PRETTY NEAT, HUH?

((BURP!))

**The same exact facial outline can be used
to draw an old man and a baby.**

# KEEP YOUR CHIN UP– OR DOWN!

Here are two examples of how easily we can add years to faces by adding a broader chin.

2 TO 5 YEARS

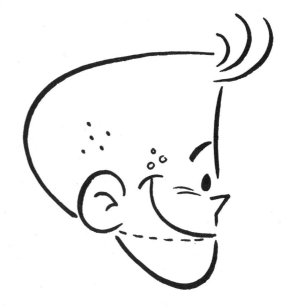

7 TO 11 YEARS

5 TO 10 YEARS

12 TO 16 YEARS

# CARTOON BODIES

GOOD CATCH!

This guy is approximately 3 heads tall,
and appears to be 6 to 8 years old.

# NICE VOICE!

**4 heads tall**

**8 to 10 years old**

**Simple rule of thumb (or, uh, "head"):
The more heads tall, the older the person.**

**This teen is about 5 to 6 heads tall.**

**Notice the extra effect of musical notes.**

This bowler was built up from the classic "stick figure,"
which is still a good way to create a cartoon body.

**Notice the "motion lines" behind his feet.**

See how the cartoon bodies look in relation to each other.

This toddler's arm is stretched up to meet the woman's hand, which is all the way down. Also, it appears that the child takes about three steps to every one of the adult's. All of these things should be considered when drawing contrasting characters like these.

# CLOWNS ARE PEOPLE, TOO!

# WELL . . . SORT OF!

# PERSONIFICATION

The main reason why I love cartooning so much is because you can do things that can't be done . . . like give life to inanimate objects!

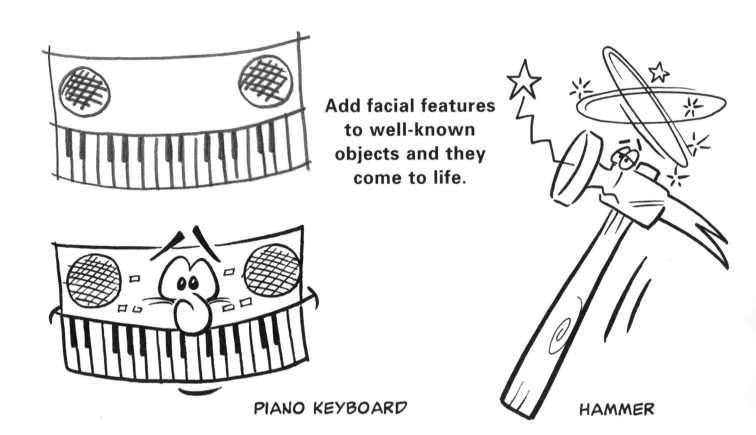

Add facial features to well-known objects and they come to life.

PIANO KEYBOARD

HAMMER

Look at the object to see what could work for the nose (as on the hammer) or teeth (as on the piano).

This waste can is just happy to help!

A soda can and a bottle going for their last walk.

RECYCLE PLANT

A storm cloud gets busy.

WOOOOOOSH

THINK OF OBVIOUS SITUATIONS FOR YOUR OBJECTS TO BE IN.

I'M STUCK!

Push pins get pushed.

JUST LOOK AROUND FOR INTERESTING IDEAS.

# COMIC BOOK HEROES

## CARTOON STYLE     REALISTIC STYLE

FRONT

As you can see, the features on the character
on the right are a bit more refined or realistic than on
his exaggerated comic counterpart.

SIDE

# CARTOON STYLE

# REALISTIC STYLE

FRONT

SIDE

# HERO FEATURES

Mix and match the following features to create
heroes, villains, and a supporting cast.

EYES

MOUTHS

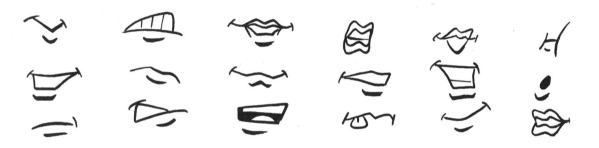

NOSES

HAIR AND FACIAL OUTLINES

# FEMALE HERO HEADS

# VILLAINS

# SUPPORTING CAST OF CHARACTERS

These are the characters that help to tell your "comic book" story. It's fun to draw a face, see how it turns out, and make up a background to go with that face.

**STERN HIGH SCHOOL PRINCIPAL**
He may have some secrets about his past.

**SECRETARY OR NEIGHBOR**
This character likes to gossip.

**THE HERO'S FRIEND**
He may one day be a crime fighter, too.

**COUNTY CORONER OR DISTRICT ATTORNEY**
He needs a shave after working overtime to crack the case.

**INSURANCE MAN OR RETAIL MERCHANT**
He asks too many questions.

**ATTRACTIVE CORPORATE EXECUTIVE**
She has a talent for helping to solve the crime.

**COLLEGE STUDENT**
She may be working towards a degree in criminology.

**CROOKED POLITICIAN**
He is known to associate with criminals.

**EX-HIGH SCHOOL FOOTBALL STAR**
He is now the local gym teacher.

# CARTOON PORTRAITS

THESE ARE ALSO KNOWN AS "CARICATURES." IT'S A CARTOON FACE OF A SPECIFIC PERSON . . . SO IT HAS TO LOOK LIKE THAT PERSON. BUT THERE SHOULD ALWAYS BE AN ELEMENT OF HUMOR, TOO!

THAT'S ME!

PRACTICE FROM PHOTOS . . .
. . . OR FROM LIVE SUBJECTS.

Try to determine the general shape of your subject's face—square, oblong, triangular, round . . . whatever! Then loosely draw that shape and begin "roughing in" the features.

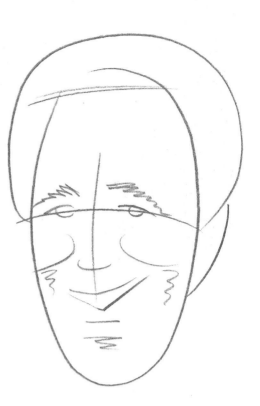

Most people don't have perfectly symmetrical faces: that is, both sides never match exactly. So it's a good idea to "play up" the person's features to give your cartoon portraits more personality. This guy, for example, has a very expressive smile.

Try to look for an overall theme for your subject. In this case, you can see sharp angles that taper down to a delicate chin.

## 3/4 VIEW

Be loose when drawing curly hair. Give your pencil its freedom to wander around within the shape of the hair!

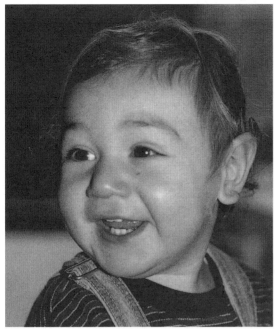

It's a bit tricky achieving the likeness of a cute little baby. Remember to keep those cheeks round and be careful not to draw the chin line too low.

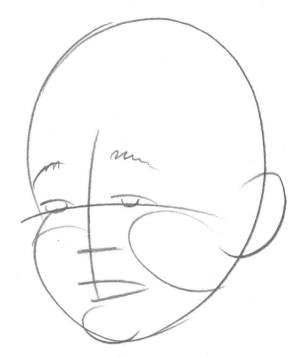

## 3/4 VIEW

Leave out most of the details inside the mouth, like the space between the top and bottom teeth. Remember, this is a cartoon! Simply *suggest* teeth, as I have done here.

This subject's bright smile make her cheeks round out and her eyes come alive.

**FRONT VIEW**

It's best to work with smiling people—when facial muscles are used, the features become prominent and the subject becomes much more interesting.

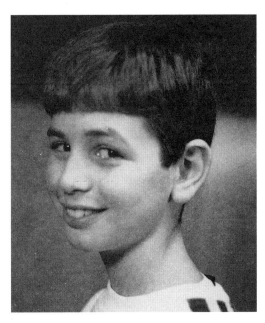

I worked from the hair down to "block in" the basic shape for this alert-looking guy.

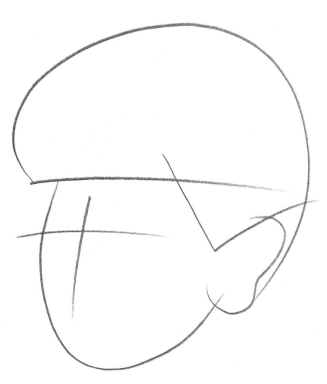

3/4 VIEW

One line is all that's needed to indicate his front teeth.

# FRONT VIEW

A happy expression makes this young girl a terrific subject! Her cheeks are an important feature, so be sure to highlight them.

# SIDE VIEW (PROFILE)

Drawing profiles is easier to do than front views
or 3/4 views because you are working with fewer features,
and you don't have to match eyes and cheeks.

**I.** Begin with the bridge of the nose and work down to the tip.

**2.** Draw in the upper lip (try to avoid making sketchy lines when working with the pen).

**3.** Then draw in the front line of the teeth and bottom lip.

**4.** Now draw the chin and part of the neck . . . and then Stop!

**5.** Next, draw two lines to outline the cheek—this is important because it tells you where to place the eye.

**6.** Draw the eye to rest on top of the cheek. Then draw the eyebrow—it is critical to the subject's expression.

**7.** Draw the outline for the head, the jawline, and the ear.

**8.** Finally, darken in the hair, add a few details . . . and there it is!

87

# MORE SIDE VIEWS

At first, try to visualize a beard as an overall shape. Then, begin to fill it in with individual pen strokes.

To the right, we have a much less detailed version of his face. There are fewer lines, bolder strokes, and a more direct approach that produces a "Cartoonified" finished product!

When working with a black marker line that is bold and strong, it is important to ease up a bit in order to draw a pretty young girl like this. Apply more pressure to the point again when you draw hair.

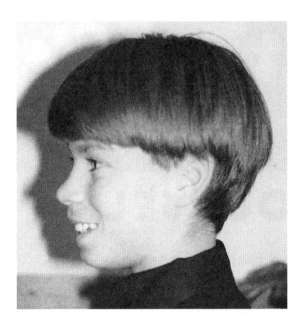

Quick-sketch portraits are usually best done directly in marker (instead of penciling first) for that spontaneous look!

People without hair are actually more difficult to draw than people with hair. This is because you only have one line to work with and it must be correct, or else the head will look odd or poorly shaped. Make sure you draw the line of the head at the correct distance from the ear, and that the ear is at the correct distance from the nose.

YOU CAN SHADE A DRAWING LIKE THIS BY LAYING A NUMBER 2 PENCIL ON ITS SIDE.

A SPECIAL THANKS TO THE FOLLOWING PEOPLE FOR KINDLY AGREEING TO BE SUBJECTS ON THE LAST NINE PAGES: LEON MALKA, WENDY PRICE, BRANDON STEINSALTZ, SUSAN RICH, RAFAEL GORDON, STEPHANIE WINER, SCOTT WOLF, JOHN ROSE, MELISSA BROWN, JASON RICH, AND FRANZ DICKERSON.

## PART 2

# ·ACTIVITIES·

NOW LET'S USE ALL THE CARTOONING SKILLS YOU'VE LEARNED SO FAR TO HAVE SOME FUN!

# EXPRESS YOURSELF!

After you've practiced drawing facial expressions on separate paper (turn back to page 41 for some hints), fill in the faces on these pages.

Be sure to notice what is going on in the scene—remember, these are the actors and you are the director! You may want to photocopy—or trace—these pictures first so you can use them over and over again.

# CHANGE ED'S HEAD

**Here's a fun way to explore lots of face possibilities!**

## THERE ARE TWO WAYS TO DO THIS EXERCISE:

1. Make photocopies of Ed's head and then add features and accessories directly onto the copies.
2. Lay a sheet of tracing paper over this page, trace Ed's head, then add features and accessories.

**Here are just a few examples of Ed's head.**
**How many can you come up with?**

# DOODLE TRICKS

# SINGLE NUMBERTOONS

There is an endless *number* (get it?) of comic possibilities.
Try these, then make some of your own.

# NUMBER COMBOTOONS

Can you find
all of the
numbers used
to create these
characters?

MAKE SOME NUMBER
COMBOTOONS OF YOUR
OWN AND SEE IF YOUR
FRIENDS CAN FIND ALL THE
HIDDEN NUMBERS!

# ALPHABETTOONS

There are twenty-six letters in the alphabet, but an endless number of doodles that you can make from each letter! Here are some examples.

# WORDTOONS

**It's fun to turn simple words into silly doodles!**

Zoo

Cow

Ann

Tony

# CHALK TALK

THIS IS A FORM OF ENTERTAINMENT THAT YOU CAN PERFORM FOR YOUR FRIENDS, FAMILY, OR IN FRONT OF AN AUDIENCE! USE CHALK OR WIDE-TIPPED MARKERS TO SKETCH CARTOONS THAT TELL A STORY OR GAG. BY THE TIME YOUR SKETCH AND STORY ARE FINISHED, YOU WILL HAVE A SURPRISE ENDING THAT ENTERTAINS AND AMAZES YOUR AUDIENCE!

# HAPPY BOY

Here is a great opening sketch to do for a Chalk Talk presentation. Remember to talk to your audience while you are telling the story. Here are some of the things you can say, but it's best when you make up your own words.

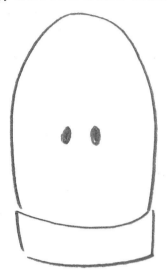

1. Let's draw a happy boy.

2. He has a big smile, and he's wearing a scarf.

3. Next we can add eyebrows and ears.

4. Now I'll draw in a head of curly hair and some texture to the scarf and collar.

5. Now let's turn this sketch upside down to see what the boy is so happy about: it's Santa Claus!

# RIDDLE

**What goes together like a bowling ball and a bowling pin?**

**Well, let's add a few lines here and there and see. . . .**

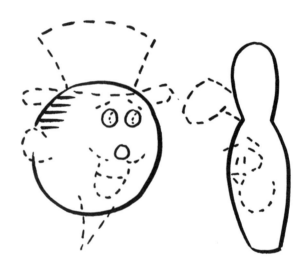

# ANSWER

**A magician and his rabbit.**

# THE RISING SUN?

**I.** Draw a mountain.

**2.** And here is the rising *sun*!

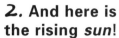

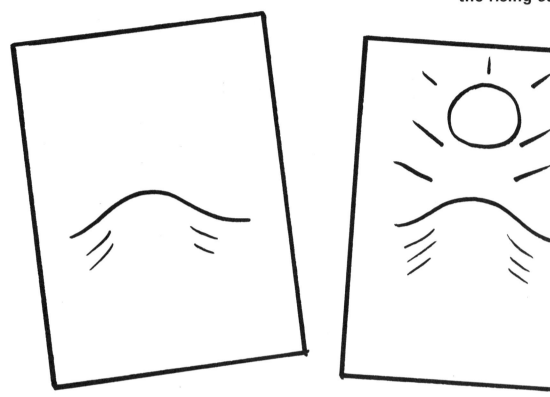

**3.** Add a boy's face and arms.

**4.** And you have the rising *son*!

# PHONE GAG

**Begin by turning to a page in your drawing pad where you have a half-drawn telephone already on the page.**

## Here's how you prepare the Phone Gag:

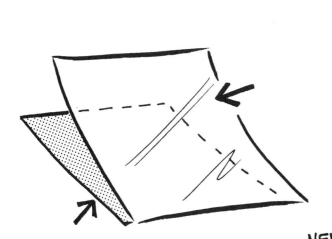

**THIN CARDBOARD ABOUT 8-1/2" X 11"**

**NEWSPRINT OR DRAWING PAPER**

**l.** Glue a piece of paper from your Chalk Talk pad onto the cardboard.

**2.** Draw *just the phone receiver* with marker, then cut it out right up to the black line.

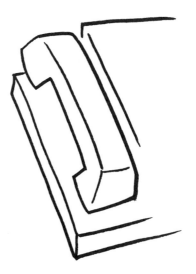

**3.** On the reverse side, roll up two very small pieces of masking tape, sticky side out, and place them as shown

**4.** Position the receiver on the paper and draw a portion of the telephone around it.

> NOTE: THE TRICK WORKS BEST IF YOU HAVE A HAND-HELD RINGER FOR A REAL SOUND EFFECT. IF NOT, JUST DRAW THE WORD "RING" WITH CARTOON EFFECTS!

 KARTOONS

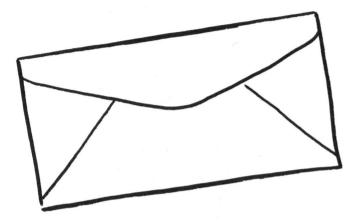

1. Draw an envelope.

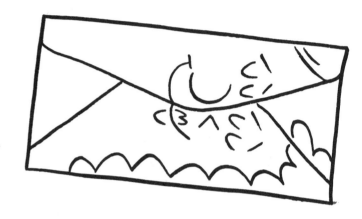

2. Next, add what looks to be meaningless doodles and squiggles. . . .

3. When turned on its side, it becomes what I call a true Love Letter!

# X MARKS THE SPOT . . .

## . . . WHERE TWO FISHES FALL IN LOVE.

# HERE IS A CASE WHERE IT WAS EASY TO . . .

## . . . MEND A BROKEN HEART!

# MOVE SY'S EYES

Here is a neat way to make an "action cartoon." Draw your own version of Sy, or copy the one on the next page.

**I.** Cut two small slits along the dotted lines in Sy's eyes, but make sure that you don't cut any paper out.

**2.** On a separate sheet of paper that is the exact width of the slits you cut into Sy's eyes, draw two wavy lines.

**3.** Insert the strip through the two slits behind the paper, then slide it up and down to see Sy's eyes move and wiggle!

**TIP:** BY FOLDING THE TOP 1/4 INCH OF THE STRIP BACK, IT WILL PREVENT THE STRIP FROM COMING OUT.

FOLD

111

# FLY SKIP'S SHIP

Using the same technique that made Sy's eyes move on the previous page, you can make Skip's ship appear to jet through outer space!

I. Cut two straight slits along the lines where indicated on the next page.

2. On a separate strip of paper that is the exact width of the slits you cut behind the spaceship, draw speed and motion lines along with little stars and asteroids.

3. Insert the strip through the two slits behind the paper, turn the sheet of paper on its side, and pull the strip through to fly Skip's ship!

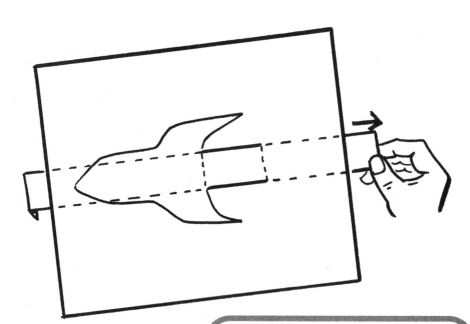

TIP: BY FOLDING THE TOP 1/4 INCH OF THE STRIP BACK, IT WILL PREVENT THE STRIP FROM COMING OUT. ALSO, BY TAPING TWO OR THREE STRIPS TOGETHER, YOU CAN HAVE A LONGER FLIGHT!

FOLD

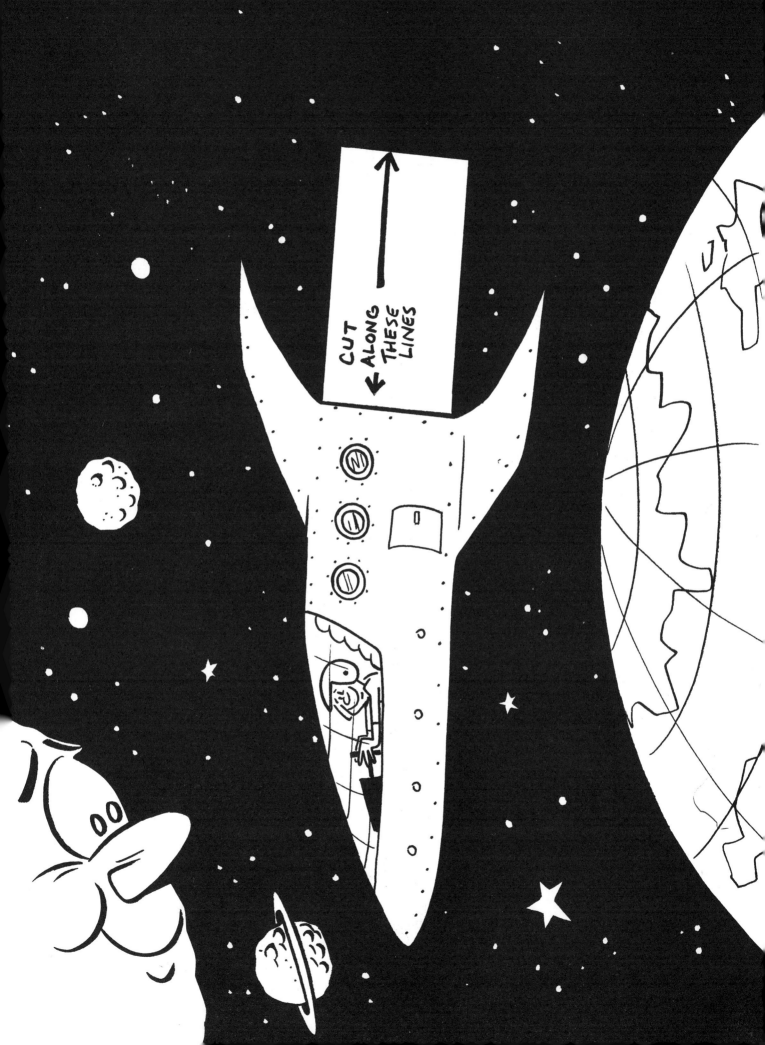

# CREATE YOUR OWN "CONNECT THE DOTS" PICTURES

**1. Draw a snappy cartoon of something.**

**2. Place a piece of tracing paper over the drawing and plot the drawing in dots. Number each dot as you draw it, and make sure that the numbers do not get in the way of the line.**

**3. It may be necessary to draw in some elements of the sketch, such as the glasses and ruffles on the shirt.**

MAKE COPIES AND GIVE THEM TO FRIENDS TO START CONNECTING.

# TRY THIS ONE YOURSELF!

# FOLD-A-FACE GAME

This is great fun at parties. You will need at least three people to play. (You'll need at least three or more people to have a decent party in the first place!)

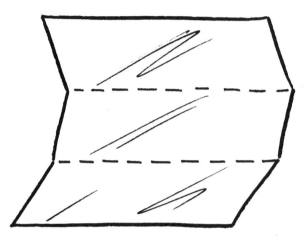

**2.** On the top third, the first person draws hair, forehead, and wacky eyebrows. Then fold this portion back so that no one can see what was drawn.

**I.** Fold a piece of paper into even thirds. Make the folds crisp.

**3.** The second person then fills in the middle portion with eyes, nose, and ears. Fold this third back to hide it.

**4.** Without looking at the other thirds, the third person then draws in the mouth and the bottom of the face.

OPEN UP THE PAGE AND WATCH THE FUN "UNFOLD!"

# LIGHTTOONS

I call these Lighttoons! Lighttoons prove that there is always more than meets the eye. (In other words, hold these pages up to the light to see the rest of the story.)

## TO MAKE YOUR OWN LIGHTOONS, FOLLOW THESE STEPS:

1. Think of a scene that will have a surprise action.

2. Draw the first cartoon on the front of the paper, making sure you leave room for the second drawing on the back of the paper.

3. Tape the paper to a window with the back facing you, then draw the surprise cartoon on the back. (Remember to write words backwards!)

# RECIPE FOR SUCCESS

# MAKE YOUR OWN
# JIGSAW PUZZLES

1. Create a drawing in marker and use crayon, colored pencils, or colored markers to color it in.

2. Next, paste or glue your work onto a piece of cardboard just thick enough so that scissors will cut through it.

3. On the reverse side, draw a pattern for the puzzle and cut the pieces out.

Of course, the more pieces you make, the more difficult the puzzle will be to put back together!

# DON'T BE AFRAID OF CONSTRUCTIVE CRITICISM ... IT HELPS TO SPEED YOU ALONG!

# SPATTERTOONS

Here is a fun way to produce an interesting effect for coloring-in selected areas of your drawings.

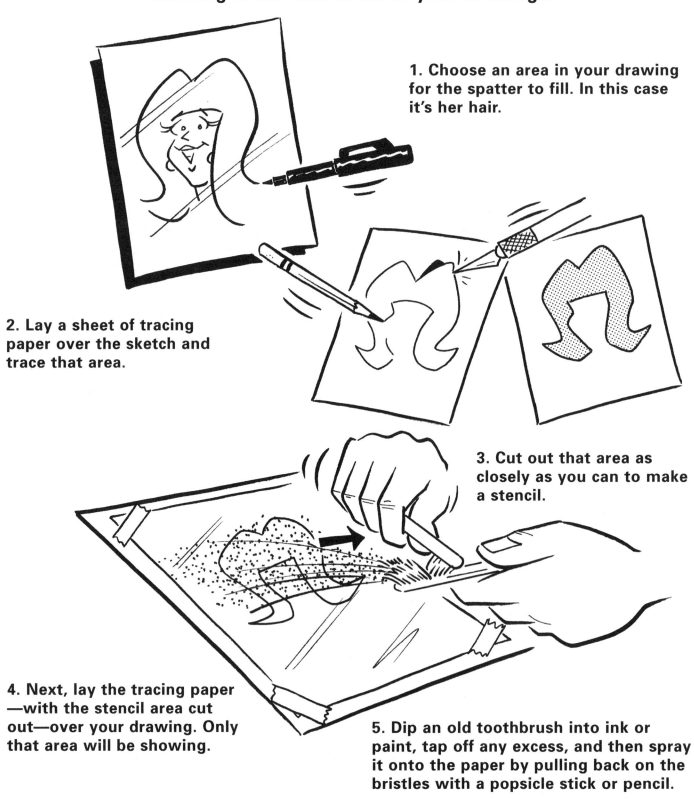

1. Choose an area in your drawing for the spatter to fill. In this case it's her hair.

2. Lay a sheet of tracing paper over the sketch and trace that area.

3. Cut out that area as closely as you can to make a stencil.

4. Next, lay the tracing paper —with the stencil area cut out—over your drawing. Only that area will be showing.

5. Dip an old toothbrush into ink or paint, tap off any excess, and then spray it onto the paper by pulling back on the bristles with a popsicle stick or pencil.

# Some Examples of Spattertoons I've Spattered!

SPATTER HAIR

## TRY IT WITH DIFFERENT COLORS

SPATTER SUIT

Here's an example where I "masked off" the main part of the drawing and spattered the background!

# CREATE YOUR OWN
# "FIND THE DIFFERENCES" PICTURES

**I.** Draw a busy scene in a box, but leave out the elements that will be different—you can add, subtract, or change things.

**2.** Next, photocopy your drawing and draw in the elements that will be different in both pictures.

**3.** Then paste the box with the new elements under the original box.

**4.** Make photocopies of the final paper—with one box on top of the other—and give it to your friends!

There are ten differences between these two pictures. Can you find them?

## ANSWERS:

1. Plug moved
2. Scissors added
3. Hair spray added
4. Picture added
5. Comb added
6. Comb is different
7. Doorknob added
8. Umbrella added
9. Flower added
10. "Open" sign added

127

THE FUN BOOK OF CARTOON FACES

Blitz